CEO
WORDS OF WISDOM

CEO
WORDS OF WISDOM

Tim Murray

CEO WORDS OF WISDOM

Copyright © 2020 Tim Murray.

All rights reserved. No part of this book may be used or reproduced by any means, graphic, electronic, or mechanical, including photocopying, recording, taping or by any information storage retrieval system without the written permission of the author except in the case of brief quotations embodied in critical articles and reviews.

iUniverse books may be ordered through booksellers or by contacting:

iUniverse
1663 Liberty Drive
Bloomington, IN 47403
www.iuniverse.com
844-349-9409

Because of the dynamic nature of the Internet, any web addresses or links contained in this book may have changed since publication and may no longer be valid. The views expressed in this work are solely those of the author and do not necessarily reflect the views of the publisher, and the publisher hereby disclaims any responsibility for them.

Any people depicted in stock imagery provided by Getty Images are models, and such images are being used for illustrative purposes only.
Certain stock imagery © Getty Images.

ISBN: 978-1-6632-0732-6 (sc)
ISBN: 978-1-6632-0822-4 (e)

Printed in the United States of America.

iUniverse rev. date: 10/08/2020

CONTENTS

Foreword vii
Acknowledgments ix

Chapter 1   You Never Get a Second Chance to Make a First Impression 1
Chapter 2   You Can Always Do More than You Think 6
Chapter 3   Success is Where Preparation and Opportunity Meet 11
Chapter 4   Perception is Reality (Whether You Like It or Not) ... 18
Chapter 5   Tomorrow Will Be Different Than Today 22
Chapter 6   What Makes You Successful at One Level is Not What Makes You Successful at the Next 27
Chapter 7   Make Decisions as if it is Your Own Personal Money 33
Chapter 8   The Best Communication is Direct Communication 38
Chapter 9   Never Hire or Promote Someone You are Not Willing to Terminate Later 44
Chapter 10   Treat all Feedback as a Gift 49
Chapter 11   Plan Your Work and Work Your Plan 54
Chapter 12   Coaching is a Gift that Must be Returned 58

Conclusion 65
Picture Gallery 67

FOREWORD

As an avid reader, I have often been asked when I will write a book. When I was working as a corporate CEO, I never had the luxury of extra time to take on such a project. However, my career transition at the end of 2019 along with the great "COVID pandemic" of 2020 provided me a golden opportunity to seize on this initiative.

In July of 2019, I finished a twelve-year career working in the small island kingdom of Bahrain, just off the east coast of Saudi Arabia. I spent that time working for a company called Aluminium Bahrain, better known as Alba, in the role of CEO for 7 of those years. Alba is one of the largest aluminium smelters in the world, with sales of US$ 2.5 billion in 2019. In addition, Alba employs around 4,000 full-time workers and the aluminum industry accounts for approximately 12% of the country's GDP.

My hope with this book is to translate my personal experiences into practical advice that can be used in everyday life. The history of the term "WoWs" (i.e. Words of Wisdom) goes back to the early days of my time as Alba's CEO. My former Public Relations team designed many types of materials to be used in ongoing training campaigns. As part of this, they came up with the idea of using a bookmark as a platform to spread my various management philosophies.

Ultimately, the bookmarks proved to be a far more powerful communication tool that I had ever imagined. The WoWs bookmarks became so popular that we would give them away at all company events. Employees would collect them and even take them home to their families. I often encourage people to read and give books to them, and there is no better way to add a personal touch than by including a custom bookmark.

There is a good chance you will recognize some of these WoWs. Many may seem like common sense, but in my experience, common sense is not very common in the business world. The stories that I used in the book are based upon events which happened in my life. I hope the lessons and takeaways from these stories can benefit you and your career, and perhaps lead you on the path to one day becoming a CEO.

ACKNOWLEDGMENTS

There are many people I would like to thank for their support in writing this book, the most important being my wife Shana, who has travelled the world in support of my career. She has provided invaluable support during the many ups and downs of life, and I would not be the person I am today without her love and guidance.

I would like to thank my parents and maternal grandparents who played a major role in my upbringing. I would also like to thank the mentors in my life, listed in chronological order of my meeting them: Jerry Habegger, Paul Larkin, Chris Bourk, Gary Shankman, John Skladan, Mutlaq Al Morished, His Excellency Shaikh Daij bin Salman Al-Khalifa and Jack Futcher. I would also like to thank my editor Jacob Rousu for his valuable contributions.

I am grateful to the Alba Board of Directors for the opportunity they gave me to be Alba's CEO. I would also like to thank all of the Alba employees and contractors that I worked with during my career in Bahrain. We were able to achieve amazing things in Safety and Production, in addition to the $3 billion Line 6 Mega-Project.

I feel fortunate to have had the opportunity to live in Bahrain, which I will always consider my second home. Bahrain was a wonderful place to raise a family and I would like to thank the leadership of Bahrain under His Majesty King Hamad bin Isa Al-Khalifa, His Royal Highness Prime Minister Prince Khalifa bin Salman Al-Khalifa and His Royal Highness Prince Salman bin Hamad Al Khalifa the Crown Prince, Deputy Supreme Commander and First Deputy Prime Minister for making Bahrain such a great country.

I am better person as a result of living overseas and I have a very different perspective than most Americans. I consider myself an Ambassador of Bahrain and I do my best to tell the true story of the Middle East in the hopes of countering the negative perceptions often reported in the news.

Now on to the stories!

CHAPTER 1

YOU NEVER GET A SECOND CHANCE TO MAKE A FIRST IMPRESSION

"Don't come here if you want to be the Finance guy"

My experience with this philosophy goes back to a job interview I had when I was twenty-nine years old. I was interviewing to be the Director of Finance at Atlantic Research Corporation (ARC). The position was in Knoxville, TN working in the automotive division. The company had two divisions: one made rockets for the US Military while the other made air bags for the automotive industry.

At the time I was the Accounts Receivable Manager, a true "bean counter" working in ARC's corporate office in Northern Virginia. A promotion to Director of Finance would be a major step-up from my current position. On paper I was not qualified for the job as I had no manufacturing experience and had always worked in a corporate office job. Going into the interview process, I had to be realistic that I was a long shot.

The day finally arrived for my big interview with Mr. John Skladan, the President of ARC's Automotive division. I had flown to Tennessee the day before and had arrived thirty minutes early for my interview. The plant was located in the industrial part of town and was intimidating coming from the corporate Ivory Tower.

John was a big guy, and I felt tiny as his hands engulfed mine in a handshake. I vividly remember coming into his office. It was as sterile as a hospital room, with no warm and fuzzy pictures in sight. He met me at the doorway and pulled me into his office. I had heard he was a no-nonsense kind of guy, and this did nothing but affirm that view.

I felt ready for the interview. I was in my best banker suit, ready with my folder of information about airbags. John immediately cuts to the chase and said "I know you are a young guy without much experience, but I've heard good things about you from the people in the corporate office. I'm willing to give you a chance, but I have a condition. ***Don't come here if you want to be the Finance guy.***"

John then went on to say that he only wanted business guys working for him. Needless to say, I was in shock and not sure what to say. That concluded my five-minute interview with John Skladan when I was told I got the job. He then called to his secretary and said that young Mr. Murray is ready for his plant tour.

As I walked down the hill from the Admin office to go on my plant tour, I thought about what just happened. I interviewed for the Director of Finance position, and this man told me not to come here if I wanted to be the finance guy. Did I really want to move my family here and work for this crazy guy?

Ultimately, I took the job and it ended up being one of my best decisions. John was a great mentor and like a second father to me. I spent seven years working directly under John, during which he demanded the very best from me. It took a few years and a lot of patience but John ultimately transformed me into that "business guy" he wanted.

As you go through life, people will make instant judgements on you based upon that first impression. You may say this is not fair, but honestly, life has never been fair. First impressions are absolutely critical, and you never know which one may change your life. When I talk about making a good first impression, it goes to basic personal hygiene (e.g. combing your hair and brushing your teeth), being dressed properly, a firm hand shake and making good eye contact.

If you are having a planned meeting, take the time to Google the person you are meeting. There is a tremendous amount of information at your fingertips. For example, go to Google and type in "Tim Murray Alba" and see how much information comes up about me.

<u>Chapter Takeaways: "You Never get a second chance to make a first impression":</u>

- Always be ready to make a good first impression.
    - You never know who is watching or who you are going to meet.
    - You will be instantly judged, and it is very hard to change a first impression after the fact.

- You need to work hard no matter what job you are doing.
    - o This is very important early in your career. If I had not done a good job as Accounts Receivable Manager, I would have never been given a chance to interview with John.
- For any job interview, be over prepared and dress for success.
    - o Never be late for a job interview
- You never know when you will find a mentor in your life but when you find one embrace the opportunity and let them be tough on you.
    - o The toughest coaches are the best coaches, they make you better.

CHAPTER 2

YOU CAN ALWAYS DO MORE THAN YOU THINK

"Just do it, there will never be a good time"

I love to use this phrase to challenge people and get them out of their comfort zones. Usually the first reaction to any large undertaking is to say "It can't be done" or "I have too much on my plate". It is human nature to hold back and avoid making commitments. However, I feel that if you don't stretch yourself, you hinder your own development.

I encountered this directly back in 2001, when my family moved to Tennessee and my son Ethan was born. I was thirty at the time and considering studying for a Master's in Business Administration (MBA). This was a huge commitment in terms of time and money, and I was still relatively new in my role as Director of Finance. I felt it would be an important step for my career and round out my skills. I had a long discussion with John about the pros and cons of the situation. I needed the company to sponsor me and allow me the necessary time off to attend the program which partly fell on normal working days. I was looking into the "Executive MBA" program, which would allow me to get an MBA while I worked. The program allowed for a full day of classes on alternating Fridays and Saturdays over a two-year period. This was a huge commitment on top of an already busy work schedule, and it would mean more time away from my wife and infant son.

After getting John's blessing, I had to then get the final approval from the boss at home. My wife, Shana, had always been supportive of my career wherever my job has taken us. At this point, we had just moved to Tennessee, a place where we had no friends or family. As part of the move, Shana had given up her teaching job in Fairfax, Virginia. In the middle of all of this, she became pregnant with my son Ethan. So, there I was, asking her if I could give up nearly all of my time on weekends with her and my son, whether for classes or for homework. This would be a huge sacrifice from her.

To make things worse, I decided to go to Vanderbilt, which was a three-hour drive away from home and required me to stay overnight in hotels during class weekends. I did have the option to do the MBA program closer to home, but Vanderbilt was a more prestigious university and I felt that name recognition would help me later on in my career. As I put forward my MBA proposal to Shana, she was obviously not very happy about it. She knew that this would put more burden on her in terms of caring for our son and that she would be alone in a place where we did not have any family. But to my surprise, she was very supportive and immediately said *"Just do it, there will never be a good time"*.

I owe all the success to those ten words. Her statement "Just do it, there will never be a good time" was exactly what I needed to hear. Many life changing decisions will not come at a convenient time, but you have to find a way to make it happen anyway.

My Vanderbilt MBA journey began in the fall of 2001 and I graduated in May of 2003. As expected, it put tremendous strain on my family situation. On top of all this, Shana became pregnant with our daughter Faith while she was managing a 2-year-old Ethan. However, the MBA program was an invaluable experience and put me on the path to become a future CEO.

I truly believe people are able to accomplish much more than they think once they are forced to think through the task. When a person really breaks down a task and organizes what needs to be done, the "impossible" becomes possible. Even if the person ends up falling short of a stretch target, I think that is better for personal development than setting a goal you know you will achieve.

Chapter Takeaways: "You can always do more than you think":

- It is human nature to hold back and set goals that you are certain you will achieve.
    - o Don't set objectives you know you will achieve, set stretch targets that are beyond what you think you can achieve.
    - o Until you push yourself to the limit, you don't know your limit.

- In your career, you will need a supportive partner (e.g. your spouse) in order to succeed.
- Don't over-analyze those big "life decisions," trust your instincts and take the leap of faith.

CHAPTER 3

SUCCESS IS WHERE PREPARATION AND OPPORTUNITY MEET

"There is no final interview, they selected you"

American race car driver Bobby Unser once said "success is where preparation and opportunity meet," and it is a saying close to my heart. I am often asked what is the biggest reason for my success, and my answer is that I am always prepared and when you are prepared you are ready to make a success of any opportunity.

This philosophy came into play for me back in 2006 when I was still the CFO of ARC Automotive. We had another very tough year, and I was under extreme pressure as the CFO. For those not familiar, the automotive industry it is very difficult to manage. When times were good, things were just OK, but when times were bad, they were very bad. As a result, I was burnt out and wanted something different. I began the process of looking for another job as I wanted out of the automotive industry. However, trying to change industries after working in the same industry for many years was not easy. When I talked to recruiters, given my long experience in the industry they would tell me that I am an "auto guy" and that switching industries would be difficult.

Because of my lack of progress in the job search, I started responding to ads in newspapers and magazines. One of those ads was a blind ad (an ad that shows that a company is looking to hire someone without giving many details) from *The Economist*. The position was for a General Manager Finance & Legal, and was based in the Middle East. I had never lived overseas, but it was something my wife and I had considered doing while our kids were young. However, I think my wife envisioned something more along the lines of London or Paris, not the Middle East.

I replied to The Economist ad in January of 2006, and I received a phone call from a large recruitment firm in March. At first, I did not remember the ad. After all, I had applied for several other positions in the time since. The woman on the phone, Valerie, started describing the position until I remembered applying. She then shared that the company in question was known as Aluminium Bahrain (Alba), located in Bahrain, a country I had never heard of before then.

We had a good conversation and she explained more about Alba and the position. According to Valerie, this was the initial phone screening stage and a few candidates would be selected for further interviewing in the next couple of weeks. A few weeks became a few months, and I waited anxiously until Valerie finally called back in June. She explained I had been selected for further screening and we then began an extensive phone interview. Valerie said the team would select three or four candidates from these interviews to come to London for an interview with the CEO of the company. She said she would let me know in two weeks if I had been selected for the face to face interview. However, this again was dragged out for a couple months. I finally did hear back from her in August when she told me I was one of the final candidates chosen for an interview in September.

I scheduled a flight to London over the weekend for a Monday interview and a red-eye flight home that night so that I could be at work on Tuesday. I tried to keep this interview from everyone at ARC. In preparation for my interview, I did as much research as I could on the aluminium industry and Bahrain. I met with Mr. Ahmed Al Noaimi, a Bahraini national, who was the Acting CEO of Aluminium Bahrain (Alba). Ahmed had been with the company for thirty years, a common tenure for Alba employees.

As the interview began, Ahmed offered me a cup of tea as I explained my background and my interest in the position. He then asked me a few general questions about my experience before moving into a discussion about daily life in Bahrain. I told him that while I had never been to the Middle-East, I travelled extensively for my current job. He then asked me if I had any questions. I had many of course, but I limited it to just a few.

I first asked if there were any other Americans in the company, and he answered that there were not. At that time, he detailed, there were very few Western expats (only thirteen out of three thousand employees), and no Americans. I then asked a few general questions about the company and industry. Finally, I asked him a more probing question: what in my CV caught his attention? I was curious about how I had made it into this process. After all, I was not really qualified for the job. I had no experience in the industry and was young for the position (only thirty-five). He said that he liked my experience in the automotive industry, an industry that was difficult like aluminum. He also said that it was important to them to have a CPA and high caliber MBA, so the decision to go to Vanderbilt had paid dividends.

The whole interview was only twenty minutes, which seemed especially short given I had flown from the USA. After the interview, Valerie called and told me that I had done well. She said that, for the final round of interviews, they would select two candidates to come to Bahrain.

Two months later it is November and it was radio silence on the Alba job. I decided to call Valerie to get an update. Valerie apologized for the delays and told me that things move much slower in the Middle East than in the United States. She explained that they were in the middle of Ramadan, the Islamic holy month when Muslims fast during the day for a period of 30 days. I immediately called my wife who told me to just write this off as it was going nowhere however, she was probably also saying to herself I hope he doesn't get this job as I don't want to move 6,000 miles to live in the Middle East!

Three months passed, and I had written off the Alba opportunity. Things at ARC were going well and I had just finished a trip to China. Upon landing in Chicago, I turned on my beloved Blackberry and saw a message from Valerie. It read "Please give me a call, I have an update." It was around 8 pm eastern standard time when I saw the message (which would have been 1 am in London), so I decided I would give her a call first thing in the morning. As I drove home from the airport, I called my wife. She was very negative about the situation and said not get my hopes up and that this is probably just a courtesy call to tell me that I did not get the job.

The next morning, I was anxious as I drove to work, and I called Valerie as soon as I got into my office. She began the call by apologizing profusely about the slowness of the process and not having been in contact with me. She explained that Al Noaimi had been officially appointed as CEO and they were ready to move the process forward. At this point I was skeptical but trying to be positive. I asked Valerie about the timing for the final interviews be held in Bahrain. At this point in the conversation there was a brief pause. I braced myself for another round of stalling when I hear Valerie's response: *"There is no final interview, they selected you."*

I was stunned. I expected this to be a courtesy call to tell me I did not get the job, but instead I was being offered a job in a country that I have never been to, in an industry I had never worked in. She explained that they would like me to visit Bahrain before I make a final decision, but the job was mine. I played it cool with Valerie and told her that I would need to discuss this with my wife.

I immediately called Shana, who thought I was joking. She was obviously upset about having to move from the hills of Tennessee to the deserts of Bahrain. However, Shana quickly said to me "You should take the job. This a once in a lifetime opportunity." Shortly thereafter, I made a trip to Bahrain and it was an amazing experience. The Bahraini people were so welcoming, and it was far more like America than I had expected. It was a good lesson in not making preconceived judgements about places you have not visited. Sadly, the perception of the Middle East is negative based upon all the false reporting in the news. At the end of the trip, I officially accepted the offer to join Alba as the General Manager of Finance and Legal.

I really feel my success in landing the Alba position goes back to preparation and hard work. When I look back at my career path if I had not worked hard as the Accounts Receivable Manager in the ARC Corporate office, I would have never been selected for the Automotive Director of Finance position. If I had not worked hard as the Director of Finance, I would not have been sponsored to get my MBA and then subsequently promoted to CFO.

When I talk about preparation, I don't mean for just a day or a week. I am talking about making preparation a constant habit, enabling you to seize opportunities when they present themselves (like the ad in *The Economist*). If I had not been prepared from a career perspective, I would not have been ready for that fateful call with Valerie and would subsequently missed out on the opportunity to later become the Alba CEO.

Chapter Takeaways: "Success is where preparation and opportunity meet":

- If you want to be successful, you must always be prepared.
- Don't be afraid to move out of your comfort zone (and possibly out of the country)
    - Don't make pre-conceived judgements about places you have not visited.
- When you live as an expat, make the most of every opportunity to travel as much as possible.
    - You may never get the same chance again.
- Early in your career, move around and take risks. You have nothing to lose.

CHAPTER 4

PERCEPTION IS REALITY (WHETHER YOU LIKE IT OR NOT)

"Finance guys are not supposed to go into the plant"

Think back to when you first started a new job, I am sure someone misjudged you which created a false perception that you did not like. Also think about how people get nicknames, often names that they don't like and that are opposite of who they are, like a big guy being called "Little John" or a slow person being called "Speedy." I know many of you will say this is not fair but once again, life is not fair.

When I moved to Bahrain the adjustment was not as easy. I had a tough time adapting to the bureaucratic state-run entity culture. Also, the sheer size of the Alba facility was overwhelming. It covered three square miles, which is three times the size of Central Park in New York City.

At ARC, I had been involved in every aspect of the business, but at Alba, I soon learned my role was to stay in my department and not ask questions. This was especially true of admin people, who were not supposed to go into operational areas. I found this strange. At ARC, admin people were always welcomed into the plant, as John Skladan wanted them to understand the process of making the product. The Alba philosophy was the total opposite. The operational people did not want people from other departments, especially finance, to learn all their tricks for fear that knowledge could be being used against them in performance reviews.

After a week in Alba, I got my official blue uniform, which was required to be worn when entering the plant. The uniform is made of heavy, flame retardant fabric. As soon as I got my new uniform, my secretary arranged plant visits for me. It had only been a few days into my reviews when the Deputy CEO (DCEO) stopped me as I was walking out of the Admin building and said "Mr. Finance guy, what are you doing in the blue uniform?" I was not sure if he was serious, so I told him that I was going into the plant for my operational training. The DCEO then proceeded to laugh and say **"Finance guys are not supposed to go into the plant."**

From that day forward, I knew that, in order to change the perception that I was just "the Finance guy," I was going to need to ruffle a lot of feathers. Ultimately, I came to understand the operations of Alba, probably better than many of the operational people. This knowledge would become invaluable when I took over as CEO. Alba at its core is an operational company, and if I was going to be successful as CEO, I needed to understand the operations.

I feel that one of the main reasons I was successful as a CEO was that I had changed the perception I was a "Finance Guy." Also, my ability to use quick math and "Own the numbers" became one of my greatest strengths when debating operational people, who love to "sand-bag." The term sand-bagging for those not familiar with it is when a person sets a very easy goal which they are sure they will achieve. The Alba operational people quickly learned that they were going to be challenged on every number they presented.

Chapter Takeaways: *"Perception is Reality (Whether You Like It or Not!)"*:

- People will create false perceptions of you based upon where you are from or your job title.
    - o This is not fair, but life is not fair, so get over it.
- If you want to understand the business, you need to understand the operations of a company.
- It is possible to change perceptions, but you will have to work hard.
    - o It will not be easy and you need to be stubborn in your approach.
- Work hard to create the "personal brand" you want the world to see, and don't let others dictate your perception.

CHAPTER 5

TOMORROW WILL BE DIFFERENT THAN TODAY

"I am pushing to put you in as CEO but don't tell anyone as it is 50/50"

"Tomorrow will be different than today" is an inspirational saying that makes a person think about how much life can change in an instant. A great example is the impact of the COVID pandemic. Could anyone have imagined the impact of this virus on the world? In January 2020, when we first heard about the COVID virus, most people called it a bad flu and said that it will go away. Then in March 2020, the entire world closed down for almost three months and the world went into a deep economic recession. As a result of this recession, forty million Americans lost their jobs. You never know how different the world can be from yesterday when you wake up in the morning.

This was especially true for me in 2012, the year I was appointed CEO of Alba. I had been with Alba since 2007, and I had a lot of success within the company. As a result of the global financial crisis in 2008, Alba went through major restructuring, reducing the number of executives from eleven people to two. I was one of the two survivors, which resulted in many opportunities for me to learn the business. As part of the restructuring, I was promoted to Chief Financial Officer (CFO), and at the same time took on the roles of Chief Marketing Officer (CMO) and Chief Supply Chain Officer (CSCO) until we recruited the people to fill these positions. Wearing three hats at once was a tremendous amount of work, but it was also sort of exhilarating, especially since that I had previously been smothered in bureaucracy.

As part of the restructuring, Alba appointed a new CEO. He was supposed to be the great turnaround artist who would save the company, but he turned out to be the furthest thing from it. The new CEO was quite arrogant and he was never accepted by the people. The company's performance deteriorated during his tenure, especially in the area of safety. During his time as CEO, Alba had five fatalities in less than three years. As a result, the Board decided to make a change, providing me with an opportunity that would flip my life upside down.

It was June 2012 and we had just finished a very tough Board meeting. The CEO had to explain another fatality to the board, and needless to say, they were furious. Unbeknownst to anyone in Alba, I was planning on going back to the US with my family at the end of that year. My contract would finish, and I was not planning to to renew it.

After the meeting, as I walked back to my office, one of the Alba Board members tapped me on the shoulder and asked if I had a second to talk. I turned around to see that was no ordinary Board member. This was Mutlaq Al Morished, the longest serving Board Director and one of the most powerful members of the Board. Mutlaq was a Saudi national and a very hard-nosed business guy. I had built a good relationship with him in the time since I joined as GM of Finance, and he was as an important mentor in my life.

Mutlaq pulled me to the side and said "I am fed up with this French CEO and all of his excuses" and he then went on to say: *"I am pushing to put you in as CEO but don't tell anyone as it is a 50/50 chance."*

I was stunned. The current CEO had only been in Alba for two years, it would be highly unusual to remove him so quickly. Then I asked myself "would they really appoint a forty-one-year-old finance guy? Am I ready to be CEO of a multi-billion company? Do I want to be the CEO of a company where people are dying?"

I immediately called my wife with the news who was shocked and went on to interrogate me, asking who is this Mutlaq guy and what was meant by the "50/50" comment. She asked me what will happen and I told her, truthfully, that I had no idea.

I waited patiently for three months to see if Mutlaq could deliver on his "50/50 promise". Fortunately, Mutlaq did deliver and I was appointed as CEO on the first of October 2012. I was CEO of Alba for an amazing seven years, and am very proud of what we were able to achieve during my tenure. Without a doubt, my biggest achievement was the transformation of the safety culture in the company. There were no fatalities during my time as CEO.

In July 2019, we completed the $3 billion Line 6 expansion project on-time and significantly under budget, which transformed Alba into the largest smelter in the world, excluding China. Upon completion of the Line 6 project, I officially stepped down as CEO as part of a planned transition to reunite with my family, who had returned home for my children to attend high school in the US.

Chapter Takeaways: *"Tomorrow will be different than today"*:

- Don't make grand plans about your career, especially when you are young.
    - I was ready to walk away from Alba and instead got the opportunity to become CEO of a multi-billion company at the age of forty-one.
- There is nothing more important than the safety of your people, if you get safety right everything else falls into place.
- As the saying goes "We are all one step away from humility" which the former Alba CEO learned the hard way.
- Remember to trust your instincts, embrace crazy opportunities and never look back!

CHAPTER 6

WHAT MAKES YOU SUCCESSFUL AT ONE LEVEL IS *NOT* WHAT MAKES YOU SUCCESSFUL AT THE NEXT

"Tim, I think we just had another fatality"

"What makes you successful at one level is *not* what makes you successful at the next" is one of the most important pieces of advice I have to give. This advice should be used throughout your whole career and becomes extremely important when you are the boss making hiring and promotion decisions.

I first heard these words back in 1999 right after being promoted to the Director of Finance. Upon receiving the news about the promotion, I was worried about the new role and having to move from Virginia to Tennessee. The next day, the CFO of the company requested to see me to congratulate me and give me his thoughts on the transition.

As I walked into his office, he congratulated me with a big smile. We had a good discussion about expectations and then at the end of the meeting he told me to "remember what makes you successful at one level is not what makes you successful at the next."

He went on to say that being in a managerial role is very different than being a "doer" and he has seen many people fail in making this transition. He said that I must to rely on my subordinates to get the job done. Managing people is a very different than being an individual contributor where you control your own destiny. When you are a manager, you have to trust others and there will be times when you get burned. However, to be a successful manager, you must delegate the work to your team and hold people accountable for their shortcomings.

The CFO's advice stayed with me throughout the rest of my career. It would become especially pertinent during the dark days of safety in Alba. It was September 2011 and I was CFO at this time, the weather was consistently above 100 degrees Fahrenheit and very humid. It was 7 am and I was driving to work when I got a panicked call from the COO. His voice was shaky as he tried to explain that there was a serious issue in the plant. I asked him to slow down and what was the issue, then he said ***"Tim, I think we just had another fatality."***

My heart jumped into my throat. My hands started shaking as I gripped the steering wheel. I told the COO that I would meet him at the accident site as soon as I arrived at the plant. I drove directly to the Carbon department where we make the large carbon anodes blocks that are used in the smelting process. It is a tough area due to the nature of the work and each block produced weighed about 1,000 pounds. In addition, the Carbon department always looked dirty due to the black carbon dust everywhere which was a byproduct of the manufacturing process.

I got out of the car, my heart pounding, my forehead covered in sweat. I walked into the plant, feeling my blood pressure go up as I approached the accident site. As I entered the area, people were scrambling as the Safety & Medical teams did their investigations. I felt my stomach drop when I saw the worker, pinned down by scaffolding. As I was stood there helpless, I kept thinking that this couldn't be happening. I felt angry and powerless as I looked upon the deceased worker, knowing this was someone's husband, father, son and brother who, in an instant, was gone. It was a horrifying experience and one that still haunts me to this day. It was one of the most painful experiences of my life, and one that could have been avoided.

One year later right before I was appointed CEO, we had another fatality. So here I am, the new CEO at the young age of forty-one, and all I can think is "who is going to die next?" Every night, I would put my phone on the nightstand and pray that no one would die as I slept.

I thought back to the advice I had received many years ago. I had to change my mindset from being a CFO to being a CEO, a CEO who was going to stop people from dying in his plant. This was easier said than done, since my ego kept telling me that it couldn't be that hard to be a CEO. Well, being a CEO is that hard. When you're a CEO, you are the one responsible for everything, there is no one else to blame. You are the guy at the top, and every decision made in the company is your responsibility.

As the new CEO, I needed to find a way to motivate the employees and get their buy-in to fix safety. The first thing I did as CEO was to terminate the company's safety consultants. They weren't necessarily bad consultants, but the company had to take ownership of safety. We had become reliant on the consultants for just about everything and safety had become a "check the box" exercise. As the new CEO, I had to shake up the organization and show that I was serious about safety. The decision to terminate the consultants sent shockwaves through the plant. Even my executives were against the decision. They told me not to do this now, that I would get blamed if something happens, but I knew it had to be done. After this day, everyone knew that safety was going to be my number one priority.

In the holy Quran, there is a verse that says that "change starts with belief." We used this saying in many of the safety campaigns to remind everyone that if we were going to change the safety culture of the plant, we had to believe in what we were doing. Getting the employees and contractors to believe in safety was not an easy task. We allowed the consultants to run the show for the last two years, but we changed this by taking ownership of safety and through our constant plant visits and campaigns using direct communication to deliver the message to all workers. This was not an easy process. In my first year as CEO, I spent around 70% of my time on safety. At the beginning, people were skeptical, but after eighteen months of constant pressure, we saw a drastic improvement in safety behavior.

We still had injuries but the number was dramatically lower and there were no more fatalities. We had changed the safety culture from a "check the box" mentality to the company's number one priority. I am very happy to state that Alba did not have a single fatality during my 7 years as CEO, and that the great safety performance has continued under the new CEO. Safety remains the number one priority in the company, and Alba has become the benchmark for safety within the aluminium industry. I consider the transformation of the Alba safety culture as my biggest achievement as CEO.

Chapter Takeaways: *"What makes you successful at one level is NOT what make you successful at the next":*

- Moving from a "doer" role into a "manager" role is not an easy transition.
    - You have to shift your mindset and not rely on what made you successful in the past.
- Be humble when you get a promotion and don't let your ego get the best of you.
- As a leader, sometimes you have to take drastic actions to get people to believe in you.
- Safety should always be the number one priority and the tone must come from the top!

CHAPTER 7

MAKE DECISIONS AS IF IT IS YOUR OWN PERSONAL MONEY

"You are in the business of making money and you are in the people business"

I very much enjoy teaching my university students this concept. During the first class, I will go around the room and ask all the students a simple question: "when you work for a company, what are you in the business of doing?" Of course, I get many altruistic answers, such as "to help people or make the world a better place" or "to save the environment."

After I have let everyone answer, I enjoy bursting their bubble by telling them that they are in the business of making money. Now, before you start calling me Gordon Gecko from the movie "Wall Street" (a movie that you should take the time to watch, you can learn many valuable lessons about the business world from doing so) and remembering his famous speech about how "greed is good," ask yourself why you go to work every day. Why did you spend so much money on your education? Why do you strive to get that big promotion? The answer is that you want to be successful and make more money.

This concept about making decisions as if it was my own money was drilled into my head by John Skladan. He would constantly tell everyone treat the company's money as if it was their own. Being the Director of Finance, I was the gatekeeper of the money, and everyone that would come to John seeking approval to spend money were immediately directed to me. John would say "if Mr. Murray approves it, I am fine with it." This, of course, put a tremendous amount of pressure on me and created lots of conflicts with everyone in the company. However, this was also a big part of my training. I was given a great responsibility, and with responsibility comes accountability. I took my role as the gatekeeper very seriously and it forced me to really learn every aspect of the business as I was not going to approve money unless I understood the purpose.

However, there was another side to John: he was also a believer in taking care of his people. John had another saying, one even more important than the one about saving money: "you are also in the people business." For a company to be successful, you must have good people running it. John believed in training and development, and he dedicated much of his time to these efforts. He believed the best way to motivate and retain your people was to help them develop themselves.

Let's combine the two parts of John's philosophy in to one magical phrase: ***"You are in the business of making money and you are in the people business."***

I am sure you are saying this is common sense, however my experience is that most people are just pushing paper and don't challenge how a company's money is spent. This is especially true in big corporations and the government. However, when it comes to your own money, I am sure you think long and hard before you pry open your wallet. Why is the decision so different? Because it is your money and once it is gone, it is gone.

To further hammer home this concept, I like to use the example of buying a car. Before you go to the car dealer, how much do you research? After you go for a test drive, why do you tell the salesmen that you are not ready to buy? Why do you wait until the last day of the month to close the deal? You go through this hassle because it is your money.

When people came into my office to get approval to spend money, I always asked them: "if it was your own personal money, would you do it?" The initial reaction was usually one of hesitation, which told me they had not really thought about why they were spending this money. Most people are quick to spend the company's money because it is not their own, but it becomes a much different decision if they consider what they would do if it was their own money.

Lastly, ask yourself this question: "what happens if your company does not make money?" The first thing they do is cut your benefits, then your salary and then your job. So, if you like having a salary and bonuses, be happy you work for a company that makes money and remember to treat it like your own money!

Chapter Takeaways: "Make decisions as if it is your own personal money":

- You are in the business to make money.
    o Never forget this and never apologize for it.
    o Always ask yourself "if it was my money would I do it?"
- Remember doing what is in the best interest of the company is in your own best interest.
- It is a good thing to work for a company that makes money
- You need to take care of your people, cutting cost will not lead you to success

CHAPTER 8

THE BEST COMMUNICATION IS DIRECT COMMUNICATION

"We have to forget what happened. We will be measured on the recovery"

I truly believe that being a good communicator is one of the most critical success factors for any leader. The more that you can directly communicate with your people the better. While you may think it will be faster to use the chain of command and have other people disseminate a message, the reality is the message will get diluted the more layers it goes through.

I learned exactly how important this philosophy was in April 2017, when Alba's entire facility had a blackout. This had never happened before and it was something that no one thought was possible, given Alba's multiple power stations and other backup contingencies. At the time of the incident, I had just arrived in the USA for Easter break when I got a panic call from the Chief Operations Officer (COO). When he told me the extent of the situation, I started to panic. This was a disaster scenario for a smelter and would result in the biggest crisis of my career.

Smelting is a continuous flow operation where there are many "pots" producing molten metal on a consistent basis at a temperature of 960 centigrade (1,760 degrees Fahrenheit for my fellow Americans). Aluminium smelting is a process that runs continuously twenty hours a day, three hundred and sixty-five days a year. If power is lost for more than four hours, the pots will solidify (i.e. freeze). A potline freeze is the worst possible scenario in smelter operations, and it takes several months to restore everything, costing millions of dollars.

After getting off the call with the COO, my wife could see that I was upset and asked me what happened. She was in as much disbelief as I was. I then told her that I was going to have to return to Bahrain immediately. As you can imagine, this did not go over well. I had been home only a couple of days and was supposed to be there for my kids' Easter break. This was not an easy decision, but I knew that, as the CEO of the company, I had to get back to restore order. This was unlike any situation in the history of the company.

The following day, I prepared for the long trip back to Bahrain which was a 24-hour journey. I flew out late on a Friday night from Washington DC and landed in Bahrain at 10 pm the next night.

Once I landed, I immediately went to the plant, only to realize that the situation was much worse than what I had been told. As a result of the power outage, we had to shut down Alba's biggest production line, affectionately known within Alba as "Big Daddy." The nickname Big Daddy came from the fact that Line 5 was Alba's biggest production line and a major contributor to the company's profitability.

It was horrifying to walk around the line, watching the smoke rise from the pots that were beginning to solidify. That night, I walked the entire potline to assess the damage, which was no easy task given that Big Daddy is 1.2 kilometers (almost 1 mile) long. So, I was completely exhausted from the 24-hour journey, yet ready to explode from anger. But even so, I had to keep my composure in front of all the employees.

This experience put everything I had built over the past 5 years as CEO to the test. From the moment I arrived, I had to be positive even though I was terrified. It was a dire situation, and if we were unable to bring "Big Daddy" back to life quickly, I would likely be fired. You may say this is not fair as I was in the USA when it happened, but the CEO is always held responsible for every choice, incident, and accident within a company.

The first thing I had to do was calm the people down and stop the rumor mill. Bahrain is a small country and rumors that Alba was going to close were spreading. The aluminium industry represented 12% of Bahrain's GDP, with thousands of jobs tied to its success. I immediately initiated a campaign to meet with all the departments, which took several days. This was all the more painful because I was still recovering from jetlag and was not sleeping due to stress. However, I knew that direct communication was essential and that the only way to kill the rumors was for the employees to hear directly from the CEO.

The meetings were very informal. We would gather large groups in conference rooms, and I would explain what happened and what we had to do to recover. The constant message that I hammered home was ***"We have to forget what happened. We will be measured on the recovery."*** There would be a time for a post-mortem, but that was for later. We had to focus on moving forward with the recovery instead of playing the blame game. I would conclude every meeting by telling the employees that their job was to do everything they could to support Line 5. The campaign was a huge success and it rallied the troops to get us on the road to recovery.

The Line 5 recovery was a very painful process that took three and a half months to complete. As the CEO of the company, I had to micromanage the process to ensure everything stayed on track. The Line 5 recovery was a good example of a time where a leader had to step in and make it painful to get results. Over the long run, I do not believe in being a micro manager but here was a situation where we were losing $1 million per day by Line 5 not running. I had to take extreme actions to get the line back up and running as soon as possible.

The majority of the restart was done in the hot summer months which made it a difficult challenge. Imagine the impact on your productivity when you have to do the required task at an ambient temperature of 110 degrees Fahrenheit. However, the Alba team did an amazing job and completed the recovery safely and in record time.

The Line 5 recovery set the industry benchmark for a potline recovery and was ultimately turned into a ***Harvard Business Case*** (hbsp.harvard.edu) about the impact of leadership during a crisis.

Chapter Takeaways: "The Best Communication is Direct Communication":

- The more the leader can communicate directly to people without filters or layers the better.
    - o   In a crisis, the leader must over communicate and be positive.

- As the boss, sometimes you have to micro-manage to get results.
    o   Sometimes you have to make it painful for the pain to go away.
- In times of crisis don't waste time looking back at what happened.
    o   You need to look forward and not cry over the split milk

CHAPTER 9

NEVER HIRE OR PROMOTE SOMEONE YOU ARE NOT WILLING TO TERMINATE LATER

"I will give some advice, go after the big fishes"

The idea that you should never hire or promote someone you are not willing to terminate later may sound harsh, but it is still a very important lesson. I learned this in my first job, and I didn't realize what a valuable piece of advice I had been given at the time.

I was working as a staff accountant for a small, family-owned business. As with most family owned businesses, there were strange dynamics within the company. In this case, the President (and owner) of the company hired his sister-in-law to be the CFO of the company. The CFO was a tough business lady who would often clash with the President about the amount of open credit allowed to be given to customers. The President was a classic sales guy who wanted to make the customer happy, whereas the CFO was the person responsible for making sure the customer paid on time. On the surface, this is a natural tension between Sales and Finance, a healthy check and balance. However, the situation became very tenuous, given the president's wife was the sister of the CFO.

I was with the company for two years, and on my last day, the president was nice enough to meet with me and personally thank me for doing a good job. As we finished up the meeting, he gave me an important piece of advice. "Never hire or promote someone you are not willing to terminate later," he said, "just look at this mess I have with my CFO. Despite everything, I can't terminate her because she is my sister-in-law. If you ever have to make hiring decisions, think of this situation as a lesson."

In my career, I have seen many people come and go, voluntarily and involuntarily. That goes with the ups and downs of any business and economy. As I write this book, companies in the US have laid off over 40 million people as a result of the COVID Pandemic. Sadly, employers need to reduce costs during such downturns in order to survive. I can tell you from experience that having to lay off people is one of the hardest things for a CEO to do. However, when you are going through a downsizing situation you must always keep in mind that you are doing this for the good of the overall company. I would tell people we are reducing 10% of the workforce to save the other 90% but no matter how you justify it, the experience is distasteful.

At the end of 2015, commodity prices collapsed as a result of China exporting surplus metal onto the global market. In a commodities business, the name of the game is cost. You have no control over the price. The only way for you to succeed in the long run is to be cost competitive. China consumes roughly 50% of all commodities (e.g. oil, steel, copper, aluminium) and as such has an enormous impact on commodity prices.

As a result of the severe drop in aluminium prices, Alba initiated a voluntary Early Retirement Scheme (ERS) as a way to reduce workforce cost. The objective of the ERS program was reduce the workforce by giving employees a severance package in return for a voluntary resignation. The local union was vocal in their opposition to the ERS program. Initially, they did a scare campaign and told the employees to not accept anything until they had a chance to negotiate a better deal. I was under significant pressure to achieve the workforce reduction target. I called an emergency meeting with the union. The chairman of the union was volatile at the beginning of the meeting, but I settled him down and told him that we needed to find a mutual solution and stop using scare tactics.

Ultimately, we agreed to increase the size of the severance package under the condition that the union would support management. At the conclusion of the meeting, the chairman of the union and I were talking about the best way to achieve the target. He looked at me and said **"I will give you some advice, go after the big fishes."** What he meant was go after the higher paid employees versus the low-level operators who make the minimum wage. He was right and it was a good idea as our objective was to reduce 10% of the workforce cost, not necessarily 10% of the workers. So, if we could do more with less why not.

The ERS program gained significant momentum once we had the support of the union. The ERS package was open to all employees, and as a result, we had many management people take the offer. One of those people was a member of my executive team who came to me and asked me if he should take the package. This was not an easy situation. I was close to this executive, since we had risen through the ranks together. However, I was having performance issues with him, and there were rumors that he was leaking information to the union.

I knew this was my chance to remove him, but I did not want it to seem like I was terminating him. That could have upset the union, and could be misconstrued as a power play on my part. While the timing of this executive leaving was not ideal, I knew it was manageable. My response to him was simple: I told him that it was a generous offer and that he should give it serious consideration. This kept me from directly telling him what to do, but still delivered the message that I was ready for him to leave.

The next morning, the executive came to my office to tell me that he had decided to take the ERS package. This sent shockwaves throughout the company. After all, the rumor in the company was that he was going to be the next CEO. No one had expected him to retire and everyone knew how close he was to the union. Later that same day, I bumped into the union chairman in the plant, and I thanked him for the advice. He looked at me strangely and asked what I meant. I told him that I followed his advice - I went after the "big fishes."

Chapter Takeaways: "Never Hire or Promote Someone You are Not Willing to Terminate Later":

- Downsizing is a painful experience that most people will experience during their careers.
    - o Remember the logic of reducing 10% to save the other 90%.
- Before you hire or promote a friend or relative, ask yourself this question: "Will I be able to terminate this person if things don't work out?" If the answer is No, then don't do it.
- In your career, remember that "business is business." You need to keep your work and personal lives separate.

CHAPTER 10

TREAT ALL FEEDBACK AS A GIFT

"In my twenty years in the company, you are the first person to ever give me feedback"

"Treat feedback like a gift" could be a difficult piece of advice to accept depending on the type of feedback you receive, but any time you get feedback from someone, you should feel fortunate. My experience is that most Managers do not give feedback and even when they do, they don't do it correctly which defeats the purpose of doing it.

Early in your career, you will be mostly on the receiving end of feedback as you get trained. When you are younger, you usually don't have people reporting to you. It is not until you climb the corporate ladder and get your first manager position that you get to be on the other side of the table and start giving feedback.

Moving to Bahrain was my first experience living in a foreign country, so I was very cautious about giving feedback to people. One thing I immediately noticed in Bahrain was how polite people were, and while this is a good thing, it does make it harder to give feedback. I was often afraid of coming across rude. I wanted to be very respectful and not offend people, but I had to find a way to give feedback if I was going to be successful as a CEO.

During my first year in the position, I had a particularly difficult board meeting where our Internal Audit department gave an update about serious issues they uncovered in the Fire & Safety department. They had reported on many shortcomings, the most serious of which was a significant number of inoperative fire extinguishers throughout the plant. Anyone who has been involved with a fire incident will tell what a scary thing fire is and when there is a fire you need fire extinguishers to work. This was a serious issue, especially given that Alba is a huge industrial plant with thousands of people working around molten metal and heavy equipment.

Needless to say, I was very upset after the meeting and I immediately sent a blistering email to the superintendent in charge of the fire section. In retrospect, I should have not sent that email when I was still angry, but my temper got the best of me.

The next day, the Superintendent in charge of the fire section requested to see me. Initially I told my secretary to say I was busy, but I felt bad about the email, so I agreed to meet him. As the meeting began, I prepared for the excuses and justifications as to why the Internal Audit report was wrong. I gave the Superintendent a stern look so he that knew that I was still upset. The superintendent started by apologizing and I could tell from his voice that he was truly sorry. At this point, I also changed my tone and gave him some feedback about what I expected from him and what he needed to do to improve. It was a very constructive discussion and I was glad that we cleared the air.

As the Superintendent was about to leave my office, he asked if he could say something and I braced myself for a final justification. Then he said *"In my twenty years in the company, you are the first person to ever give me feedback."*

I did not know what to say. I wondered how this was possible. In twenty years with the company, no one had ever given this guy feedback? It was an eye-opening experience for me, and one that made me realize that I had a long way to go if I was going to create a culture of feedback in the company.

As a result of this incident I really changed my approach on how to give feedback. I had to remember that the company culture was not to give feedback and it would take time to change this mindset. I also had to remember that English is the second language in Bahrain. This is not to say the English in Bahrain is not good – in fact, the standard for English is very high. However, I would often speak too fast or use slang that was not familiar to them. As I later learned when I took Arabic lessons, it was easy for things to be lost in translation when one person is speaking in a second language.

Next, I had to pick the right time to give feedback and be less blunt. However, even after adapting my style and taking these extra precautions I found it difficult to give feedback. Anytime I gave a person critical feedback, their inner ego immediately awoke and started to whisper that their boss was wrong and didn't appreciate how hard they worked.

I highly recommend that you read a great book called *Thanks for the Feedback*. The authors, Douglas Stone and Shelia Heen, give great insights into the types of feedback and advice on how to approach those difficult discussions. They categorize feedback into 3 types: Appreciation, Coaching and Evaluation (or the acronym **ACE**). This was an important lesson for me to learn and one I had never really thought about previously. A common pitfall is to give wrong type of feedback depending on the situation (e.g. coaching versus evaluation or vice-versa).

Ultimately, I feel I was able to change the feedback culture in Alba which played a big part in the success of developing and promoting people within the company.

Chapter Takeaways: "Treat All Feedback as a Gift":

- Before giving feedback, be in the right frame of mind and pick the right time of day.
    - Remember the three types of feedback: Appreciation, Coaching and Evaluation (ACE).
    - Avoid aggressive body language (e.g. crossing your arms or rolling your eyes).
- Ask yourself these 3 questions before any feedback session:
    - How would you feel if you were about to be given this feedback?
    - How should I tailor the feedback to the specific person/situation (remember **ACE**)?
    - How do I get the person to accept the feedback?
- If you are giving the feedback, you also need to be open to receiving feedback.
    - Feedback is a 2-way street, you have to be open to receive feedback about the way you give feedback.

CHAPTER 11

PLAN YOUR WORK AND WORK YOUR PLAN

"Timmy, always have a plan of the day"

Jan	Feb	Mar	Apr
May	June	July	Aug
Sept	Oct	Nov	Dec

I learned the importance of planning from my maternal grandfather, better known as Papa, who lived by the mantra "plan your work and work your plan." As a child, I spent a lot of time with Grama & Papa Speece since both of my parents had full time jobs. My dad was an insurance agent who did a lot of traveling, and my mom was a nurse who worked on shift. Papa was the king of planning. I would often hear him say "plan your work and work your plan." Papa retired at the age of 59 and lived until he was 92 and made his retirement money last 33 years.

As a little boy, I remember Papa saying to me *"Timmy, always have a plan of the day."* This was his key to success. Papa had this amazing personal organizer that he kept in his car clipped onto his sun-visor. The organizer was filled with pencils, pens, paperclips, rubber bands and, most importantly, the almighty Post-it note. Papa would always write down his plan of the day on a Post-it to ensure that he never forgot anything, and as each task was completed, he would cross it off and call it "another small victory."

For those not familiar with a "Post-it" note, it is a small piece of paper about the size of a business card that you can use to write yourself small reminders. The beauty of the Post-it note comes from the adhesive on the back of the note, so you can stick them anywhere as a reminder. Post-it notes are cheap and come in a small-blocks of 50-100, which makes it possible to use as many you want. For people like me, that means putting "Post-it" notes everywhere. I put them on my desk, briefcase, refrigerator, nightstand and even in my car.

Because of this, I like to keep Post-It on my desk and my computer monitor so they are always in front of me. I am sure my younger readers are wondering why I don't just use my smartphone. I actually do use my notepad on my iPhone, but I firmly believe that our brains work better when we physically write things down and keep them constantly visible.

When I first became Alba CEO, the hardest adjustment was managing my time. Prior to becoming CEO, I ran most of the executive functions within the company, but when you are the CEO, the demands on your time go up exponentially. Everyone wants your time: the board, the shareholders, the customers, the suppliers, the banks, the investors, the media, everyone. You are now the one in charge, and you have to make all the appearances.

You may have heard the age-old question on what the most valuable commodity is. Some would say gold, while others would say information. However, I would argue that time is the most valuable commodity and something to be treated like gold. To be successful, we need to make the most of our time as there is a limited supply. Time management needs to be managed closely to avoid the temptation of wasting especially on things like social media.

When I look back at my career, I believe that having a "plan of the day" and proper time management allowed me to achieve far more than I would have otherwise. Papa's saying about "plan your work and work your plan" is a great way to remind yourself about the importance of time management.

The simple Post-it played a critical role in effective time management and the higher I climbed the corporate ladder, the more precious my time became.

Chapter Takeaways: "Plan Your Work and Work Your Plan":

- Having a "plan of the day" is essential for effective time management.
    - o Write your plans down on a Post-it and keep it in front of you.
    - o As you complete each task, scratch it off the list (another small victory).
- The higher you climb, the more demands there will be on your time (treat it like gold).
- Time is the most valuable commodity, manage it wisely as you never get it back!

CHAPTER 12

COACHING IS A GIFT THAT *MUST* BE RETURNED

"You are ready and will know what to do"

We should never forget the impact coaching has on your success. When it is your time to be the coach, don't say that you don't have the time or that you are too busy. Someone made the time to help you, so you need to make the same sacrifice. Coaching is not something that comes naturally for most people, but it can be learned through a lot of practice and patience.

My belief in coaching comes from a lifetime of playing competitive sports, which I did all the way through university. When I was young, I was always playing sports, and there was always a coach around. The majority of coaches are volunteers, and even the ones who are paid are not paid much. We should be grateful to our coaches for their contributing many thankless hours to training us. The same applies to those people who coach us in the workplace, who also play a critical role in our career development.

I am sure many of you believe that it is only logical to give back, but most people don't want to invest the time to develop people or, even worse, they avoid it for fear that they could take their job. I have been fortunate enough to have many coaches throughout my life.

In Alba, I spent a tremendous amount of time coaching people because I believe the success of a company depends on the success of your people. The best way to motivate people and help them become successful is to educate and develop them. We often hear that "people are your greatest asset," but in my experience, most people only give this idea lip service. I like to ask these people this question: what asset walks in and out of your company every day, but may never come back? The answer is your people. In today's ultra-competitive world, talented people are in constant demand. You need to realize that your good employees can instantly leave for better opportunity. The highflyers can easily jump ship, unlike the poor performers that never leave.

In Alba, I started an MBA sponsorship program wherein the company would sponsor employees to get an MBA as part of their Training and Development Plans (TDPs). Initially, the MBA program was for people already in management roles that needed to round out their skillset. We also targeted the young highflyers who would be the future leaders of the company. When I took over as CEO, I was the only person in the management team to have an MBA. I knew I had to address this if I was going to take Alba to the next level. The majority of the management team had a background in engineering and grew up within the company. As they got promoted, their roles changed, but they were not given management training.

You may ask why engineering people need an MBA, but I believe that anyone in a senior management role should have an MBA. Alba, for example, is a giant company with annual sales of around $2.5 billion. However, when you break it down, there are many big businesses within the overall business. In fact, many of the business units within Alba would be large businesses on a standalone basis. For example, the Line 6 project added 540K metric tons in annual production, which is approximately $1 billion per year in annual revenue. Do you think the manager of a billion-dollar business needs to have MBA skills? The answer is obvious.

My final story is about my coaching experience with Mr. Ali Al Baqali, the current CEO of Alba. Ali had been with Alba for over twenty years, growing up in the purchasing department. Prior to my being promoted to CEO, I was in the role of CFO, so one of my top priorities as CEO was to fill the CFO position, and I wanted a strong numbers person. I believe that the CFO is the second most influential executive after the CEO. There is a saying that "numbers are the language of business," so the CFO had better be a good numbers person.

I am also a big believer in promoting from within the company. When you promote from within the company, it sends a strong message that you are serious about the development of your people. You want your employees to know that if they work hard, they have a chance to move up within the company. Also, when you promote from within the company, you create promotions within the management chain. My promotion to CEO is a perfect example, because once I took that position, then the CFO position opened up, continuing all the way down the management chain.

Based upon this philosophy, I decided to promote Ali to CFO from his position of Purchasing Manager, which was a big jump for him. Many people questioned my decision. After all, Ali was not a prototypical CFO. However, he did have a degree in accounting and was very good with numbers. But more important to me was that Ali had the right attitude about being developed into the role. I pushed Ali very hard to "own the numbers" and forced him out of his comfort zone. I remember seeing Ali work countless hours and being the last person to leave the office at night. In addition to his work, he was also pursuing an Executive MBA from Essec University in partnership with the French Arabian Business School. Ali was also part of the first batch of employees sponsored by Alba to enter an MBA program.

Ali was CFO for four years before being promoted to Deputy CEO in 2017. Ali was in the role of DCEO for two years as a part of a planned transition for him to take over for me upon completion of the $3 billion Line 6 expansion project. My family had moved back to the USA for my kids to attend high school, but I had agreed to stay on to finish the Line 6 project.

On my last day in 2019, I left Ali a card with some advice on the transition along with a final message: *"You are ready and will know what to do."* Ali's promotion to CEO was well deserved and under his leadership, Alba continues to have great success. Today with the completion of Line 6 Alba is now the largest aluminium smelter in the world, outside of China.

Ali's rise from Purchasing Manager to CEO is an amazing story and a great example of promoting from within a company and the power of coaching.

Chapter Takeaways: "Coaching is a Gift that MUST be Returned":

- Coaching is critical to your success in your life and in your career.
    - o You need to take an active role to find coaches, they don't just magically appear.
    - o Coaching is a thankless job and not something people get paid extra to do.
- Not all coaches will be good, but even when you have a bad coach, try to learn from them.
    - o Many people don't want to be coaches for fear of losing their job to you in the future.
- Money is not what motivates people, people want to be developed (and promoted).
    - o Always look to promote from within the company.
- When it is your turn to be "The Coach" make the time and pay it forward.

CONCLUSION

Writing a book was much harder than I expected, it was a painful, time consuming process that really challenged and, at times, frustrated me. The process pushed me out of my comfort zone, but ultimately it was a very rewarding experience.

I hope that the book provided you practical tips and tools to use in your career. The world has drastically changed because of the COVID pandemic. Many millions of people have lost their jobs and we can expect the economic recovery to be slow and painful. I think now more than ever the lessons from the WoWs can be applied to help you survive and thrive in the post COVID world.

I also hope this book ignites your passion for reading. I know most people feel overwhelmed when they are given a book to read. I believe that reading should be as enjoyable as watching TV. I often read multiple books at the same time, which is just like watching multiple shows on Netflix.

Also, before you say you are too old to start reading, I am proof that it can be done later in life. I did not find my passion for reading until my mid-thirties. When I talk to people about why they don't read, the most common response I get is that they do not have time. At that point, I usually ask them how much time they spend on their iPhone every day. I am sure you can re-allocate some time to find 15 minutes to read, which is my daily target.

If you break down a day, fifteen minutes is only 1% of the day (15 divided by 1,440 minutes). At first, the fifteen minutes a day reading habit will annoy you just like when you first started wearing a seatbelt, but within a few weeks, it will become something you do automatically.

As for me, I have now entered the world of management consulting as the Founder & CEO of Cardinal Virtues Consulting, Inc. I am also working as an adjunct professor at Susquehanna University, teaching classes on the impact of CEO leadership.

The name Cardinal Virtues go back to my Catholic high school years. For those not familiar with the Cardinal Virtues, there are four: Wisdom, Temperance, Justice, and Courage. These are principles I strive to live by every day.

If after reading this book you feel like I may be of help to you or your business, my website is www.cardvirtues.com and my email is tim@cardvirtues.com.

I also welcome the opportunity to get feedback from you about the book.

Remember to read 15-minutes a day!

PICTURE GALLERY

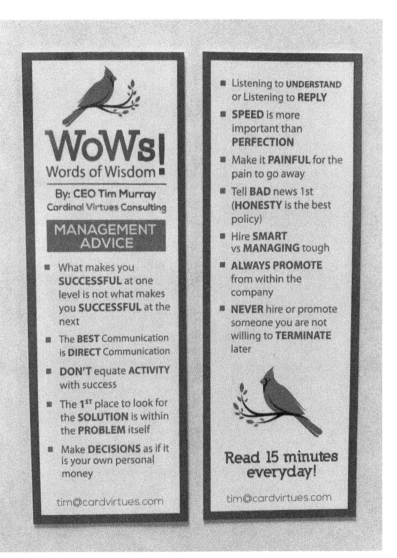

Example of WoWs bookmark on Management Advice.

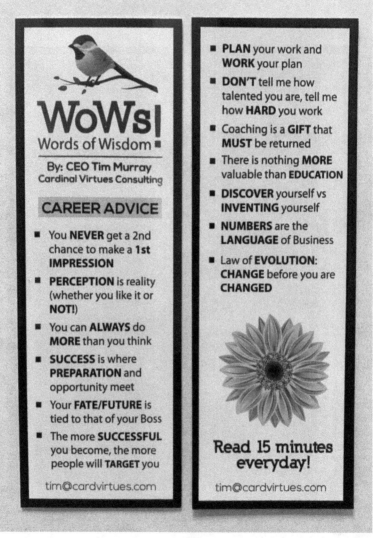

Example of WoWs bookmark on Career Advice.

My Mom (Ellen Preece) as a young nurse

Tim at age 10 with and my Dad & Coach (Jim Murray)

My maternal grandparents Margaret & Robert Speece (better known as Grama & Papa)

May 1989 Bishop O'Reilly High School graduation with my Mom & Dad

1992 Tim the ace pitcher for Susquehanna University baseball team

May 1993 Susquehanna University Graduation with my girlfriend (Shana Larkin) now wife

May 2003 Vanderbilt MBA graduation Tim holding 2-year-old Ethan & Shana pregnant with our daughter Faith

January 2006 the infamous blind ad from "The Economist" that landed me in Bahrain

April 2007 Tim & Shana celebrating my birthday right before we moved to Bahrain

September 2007 Ethan and Faith 1st day of school at St Christopher School Bahrain

April 2012 Baseball Coach Tim with Ethan and Shana at annual Dubai invitational. Note in the background you can see the top of the Burj Khalifa (the tallest building in the world).

2015 Tim and John Skladan at mentoring training session held in Bahrain

2016 Tim with Alba Board Director Mutlaq Al Morished

April 2017 painful night inspection of the Line 5 potline freeze after my 24-hour journey from Virginia. As you can see from picture I was not happy! From left to right Mohamed Al Zainal Line 5 Manager, Amin Sultan CPO, Abdulla Habib COO and Tim.

November 2017 in Washington DC when Alba was awarded the top exporter award by His Royal Highness Prince Salman bin Hamad Al Khalifa the Crown Prince, Deputy Supreme Commander and First Deputy Prime Minister of Bahrain.

June 2018 Ethan sitting in the CEO Chair during his summer internship.

December 2018 family visit to Alba, from left to right Faith, Tim, Shana and Ethan

January 2019 Tim with Ali Al Baqali then Deputy CEO of Alba. Ali was subsequently promoted to CEO upon my departue from Alba.

May 2019 Ethan with his grandparents at his high school graduation, from left to right Paul Larkin, Ellen Preece, Ethan, Charlie Preece and Alicia Larkin.

May 2019 Tim at William and Mary (WM) MBA graduation for two Alba sponsored employees, from left to right Abdul Rahman Al Mullah, Amanda Barth (WM MBA Admissions Director), Tim and Nehdal Yousif

June 2019 Tim with His Excellency Shaikh Daij
bin Salman Al Khalifa, Alba Chairman

June 2019 Tim and Faith during her summer internship

July 2019 Tim and Mohamed Khalil Saeed Alba Safety Director (the former Fire Superintendant)

July 2019 key members of the Line 6 project team. From left to right, Shawqi Al Hashimi Alba Line 6 Project Director, Denis Garrity Bechtel Line 6 Project Director and Paul Otteson Alba Line 6 Manager.

November 2019 Line 6 inauguration celebration in Bahrain under the patronage of His Majesty King Hamad bin Isa Al-Khalifa. Picture with Jack Futcher, Vice Chairman of Bechtel Corporation who was the prime contractor on the Line 6 Project.

First day at Alba (May 2007)   Last day at Alba (July 2019)

"CHANGE EQUALS OPPORTUNITY"